Serving the Call: A Training Manual for New Governance Body Members
© 2025 Keith Clark-Hoyos
All rights reserved.

No part of this publication may be reproduced, stored in a retrieval system, or transmitted in any form or by any means—electronic, mechanical, photocopying, recording, or otherwise—without the prior written permission of the author, except in the case of brief quotations embodied in critical articles or reviews.

Published by Clark-Hoyos Publishing
ISBN: 979-8-9987673-3-3

Library of Congress Control Number: [Pending]

Cover and interior design by Keith Clark-Hoyos

Printed in the United States of America

Scripture quotations are from the New Revised Standard Version Updated Edition (NRSVue), unless otherwise noted. Used by permission. All rights reserved.

This book is intended to support leaders across diverse Christian traditions. The content reflects shared practices in church governance and is not intended as legal, financial, or doctrinal advice. Always consult your denomination's policies and local regulations when implementing changes.

For bulk orders, permissions, or additional resources, please contact:
service@ChurchTrainingCenter.com

Serving the Call

Forming Faithful Leaders for Sacred Responsibility

A Training Manual for New Governance Body Members

*To the faithful board members who serve with courage and humility,
answering God's call to steward sacred responsibility.
Your quiet commitment strengthens the Church.*

*And to my beloved wife, Zulima,
whose unwavering support and love light every step of this journey.*

Acknowledgments

Thank you to the countless congregations I've served—from my early days as an intern, through my time in conference leadership, to the churches I now support through Church Training Center. Your faith, challenges, and stories have shaped this manual, a love letter to the Church's sacred work of governance.

To the Church Training Center team, your dedication to empowering leaders brings this vision to life. And to my wife, Zulima, your partnership in every trial and triumph makes this work possible. Together, we serve the Spirit's call.

About the Author

Keith Clark-Hoyos is a dedicated leader known for his unwavering positivity and remarkable ability to guide and inspire within the realm of church leadership and administration. His life journey has been characterized by a deep commitment to personal and professional growth, a passion for teaching and coaching, and a profound love for nurturing individuals and organizations toward their highest potential.

In 2015, Keith transitioned from his role as a church judicatory leader to found Church Training Center — a thriving consulting, coaching, training, and accounting firm serving churches and nonprofits across the nation. Together with his wife and partner, he has built a team that supports mission-driven ministries with clarity, care, and Spirit-led wisdom.

Keith holds a Master of Arts in Ministry, Leadership & Service from Claremont School of Theology and an undergraduate degree in Business Administration and Church Ministries from Simpson University. He is also a Daoist Monk in the Wù Zhēn Pài (Awakened Reality Sect) lineage and brings a deeply contemplative and spiritually grounded presence to his work.

At the heart of Keith's calling is a desire to empower church leaders to live faithfully, lead effectively, and align all resources — financial, human, and spiritual — with the mission God has placed before them.

Welcome to the Call

Welcome to *Serving the Call: Forming Faithful Leaders for Sacred Responsibility*, a training manual crafted for new governance body members to lead with faith and purpose. This manual, paired with *Embracing Our Call* and the Effective Church Leadership Community resources, forms a complete training system for faithful governance. Designed for Good Governance Training or Introduction to Church Leadership in the Effective Church Leadership Community, it guides you through two retreats and an Anniversary Retreat (10–17 hours) to build, strengthen, and sustain your church's mission. Retreat 1 (4–5 hours) aligns mission, roles, and meetings. Retreat 2 (4–5 hours) deepens stewardship, conflict resolution, and commissioning. The Anniversary Retreat (3–4 hours) renews leadership vitality. Prepare with *Embracing Our Call* readings. Share reflections in the Effective Church Leadership Community forums to grow together. Choose two one-day retreats, a two-day intensive, four 3-hour sessions, or eight weekly meetings. The Table of Contents and Retreat-at-a-Glance guide your journey, with the Facilitator's Guide for detailed tips. You're called to this sacred work—let's begin, guided by the Spirit.

Webinar summaries are in the Appendix, page 69, unless noted.

Table of Contents

Section	Page
Retreat-at-a-Glance	1
Retreat Guide	2
Facilitator's Guide	4
Session Planner Template	13
Retreat 1: Building the Foundation	15
Chapter 1: Serving Our Call	17
Chapter 2: Finding Our Purpose	21
Chapter 3: Leadership as Sacred Trust	25
Chapter 4: Meetings as Sacred Space	29
Retreat 2: Strengthening the Call	33
Chapter 5: Making Sense of the Numbers	35
Chapter 6: Faithful Stewardship of Church Resources	39
Chapter 7: Courage, Compassion, and Commitment	43
Chapter 8: A Benediction of Boldness	47
Anniversary Retreat: Sustaining the Vision	51
Chapter 9: Sustaining Leadership	53
Chapter 10: Governance as Covenant	57
Chapter 11: Transparency, Accountability, and Trust	61
Chapter 12: Mentoring New Leaders	65
Appendix: Webinar Summaries and Supplemental Resources	69
Effective Church Leadership Community	76
Glossary of Governance & Finance Terms	79
10 Practices of Spirit-Led Governance	80
Scripture Index	81
Leadership Rooted in Discernment	82

Retreat-at-a-Glance

This table summarizes *Serving the Call*'s 12 chapters across three retreats, helping facilitators plan sessions. Use the Table of Contents for detailed navigation or the Retreat Guide for homework and webinar details.

Chapter	Topic	Retreat	Page
1: Serving Our Call	Spiritual Governance	Retreat 1: Building the Foundation	17
2: Finding Our Purpose	Mission Discernment	Retreat 1: Building the Foundation	21
3: Leadership as Sacred Trust	Trust-Building	Retreat 1: Building the Foundation	25
4: Meetings as Sacred Space	Discernment in Meetings	Retreat 1: Building the Foundation	29
5: Making Sense of the Numbers	Financial Clarity	Retreat 2: Strengthening the Call	35
6: Faithful Stewardship of Church Resources	Budget Alignment	Retreat 2: Strengthening the Call	39
7: Courage, Compassion, and Commitment	Conflict Resolution	Retreat 2: Strengthening the Call	43
8: A Benediction of Boldness	Commissioning Leaders	Retreat 2: Strengthening the Call	48
9: Sustaining Leadership	Burnout Prevention	Anniversary Retreat: Sustaining the Vision	53
10: Governance as Covenant	Covenantal Unity	Anniversary Retreat: Sustaining the Vision	57
11: Transparency, Accountability, and Trust	Accountability Systems	Anniversary Retreat: Sustaining the Vision	61
12: Mentoring New Leaders	Leadership Transitions	Anniversary Retreat: Sustaining the Vision	65

Retreat Guide

This guide maps *Serving the Call*'s 12 chapters to three retreats, detailing *Embracing Our Call* homework and optional webinars to prepare participants. Webinar summaries (~100 words, ~1–2 minutes) are in the Appendix (page 69) for those opting not to watch the ~1-hour videos[^1]. *Embracing Our Call* chapter page numbers are in its table of contents, available in the Effective Church Leadership Community (pages 76), to aid navigation. The Facilitator's Guide (page 4) details format options (two one-day retreats, one two-day retreat, four 3-hour retreats, eight sessions) and the Anniversary Retreat structure.

Retreat	Session	Serving the Call Chapter	Homework (*Embracing Our Call*)	Webinar (Optional, ~1 hour)	Time
Retreat 1: Building the Foundation	1	Chapter 1: Serving Our Call (page 17)	Chapter 1: The Spirit Has Placed Us Here	Good Governance	60 min
	2	Chapter 2: Finding Our Purpose (page 21)	Chapter 2: Paths Made Straight	Mission, Vision & Values	75 min
	3	Chapter 3: Leadership as Sacred Trust (page 25)	Chapter 3: The Threefold Cord	Creating a Healthy Church Governance Culture	60 min
	4	Chapter 4: Meetings as Sacred Space (page 29)	Chapter 10: Meeting in the Presence of God	Leading Effective Church Meetings	75 min
Retreat 2: Strengthening the Call	1	Chapter 5: Making Sense of the Numbers (page 35)	Chapter 4: Stewarding the Storehouse	Building Financial Literacy Among Church Leaders	75 min
	2	Chapter 6: Faithful Stewardship of Church Resources (page 39)	Chapter 15: Accountability in Action	Budgeting for Church Programs	75 min
	3	Chapter 7: Courage, Compassion, and Commitment (page 43)	Chapter 23: Blessed Are the Peacemakers	Church Conflict Resolution	60 min
	4	Chapter 8: A Benediction of Boldness (page 48)	Chapter 27: Unity in Calling	Why Be Do	60 min

Retreat	Session	Serving the Call Chapter	Homework (*Embracing Our Call*)	Webinar (Optional, ~1 hour)	Time
Anniversary Retreat: Sustaining the Vision	1	Chapter 9: Sustaining Leadership (page 53)	Chapter 5: Until the Sun Set	Preventing Leadership Burnout	60 min
	2	Chapter 10: Governance as Covenant (page 57)	Chapter 9: Sealed in Covenant	Duties of Corporate Officers	60 min
	3	Chapter 11: Transparency, Accountability, and Trust (page 61)	Chapter 13: Protected by Purpose	Creating a Healthy Church Governance Culture	60 min
	4	Chapter 12: Mentoring New Leaders (page 65)	Chapter 16: Subjecting to Governing Authorities	Leadership Transitions: Succession Planning for Church Leaders	60 min

Facilitator's Guide

This guide equips you to deliver *Serving the Call* for new governance body members, whether in Effective Church Leadership Community or independent settings, forming faithful leaders for sacred responsibility. It offers flexible formats, practical tools, and tips to engage diverse groups, ensuring accessibility for novice facilitators. Together, we use *Embracing Our Call* homework (1 hour, with brief summaries in Appendix, page 69) to prepare participants, focusing 60–75 minute sessions on discussion and exercises. Share reflections and outputs in Effective Church Leadership Community forums (e.g., "How did Chapter 2's Mission Audit shape your mission?", Appendix, page 69). The Session Planner Template (page 13) and templates in the Effective Church Leadership Community (pages 76–77) streamline planning. The Facilitator's Preparation Checklist (page 11) consolidates materials and steps.

Format Options

Serving the Call uses 12 core chapters (1–12) across multiple formats to suit church boards. Homework and webinars prepare participants, while sessions foster interactive reflection and practice. Engage via Effective Church Leadership Community forums for ongoing dialogue.

- **Two One-Day Retreats (8–10 hours):**
    - **Structure:** Retreat 1: Chapters 1–4 (4 sessions, 4–5 hours); Retreat 2: Chapters 5–8 (4 sessions, 4–5 hours).
    - **Timing:** Two days (e.g., two Saturdays, 9:00 AM–2:00 PM, with 30-minute breaks after sessions 2 and 3).
    - **Use Case:** Ideal for intensive, accessible training, balancing depth and flexibility.
    - **Facilitation Tips:**
        - Use 60 to 90-minute sessions for each chapter.
        - Select 2 Group Reflection Questions (e.g., "How do we align with our Calling?" in Chapter 1) and 1 Group Practice Exercise.
        - Begin with a 2-minute prayer, using prompts like "What resonated from *Embracing Our Call*?"
        - For hybrid, use Zoom breakout rooms for exercises (e.g., Covenant Writing, Chapter 3) and polls for questions (e.g., "What sustains our board?" in Chapter 9).
        - For large groups, pair for exercises like Trust Mapping (Chapter 11).
        - Post outputs in Effective Church Leadership Community forum (Appendix, page 76, e.g., "Share Chapter 6's Budget Alignment Map").
        - Download templates (e.g., Covenant, Chapter 3; Financial Dashboard, Chapter 5) from the Effective Church Leadership Community, page 76.
        - ⏱ Optional: Skip secondary exercises (e.g., Mission Moment, Chapter 1) if time is tight.
        - **Materials:** Paper, pens, mission statements (Chapter 2), covenant template (Chapter 3), flipchart (Chapter 4).

- **One Two-Day Retreat (8–10 hours):**
  - **Structure:** Day 1: Chapters 1–4; Day 2: Chapters 5–8 (8 sessions).
  - **Timing:** One weekend (e.g., Saturday 9:00 AM–2:00 PM, Sunday 1:00 PM–6:00 PM, with 30-minute breaks).
  - **Use Case:** Suits Effective Church Leadership Community cohorts or regional retreats for immersive learning.
  - **Facilitation Tips:**
    - Use 60 to 90-minute sessions for each chapter.
    - Post in Effective Church Leadership Community forum (Appendix, page 76, e.g., "How did Chapter 7's Conflict Map foster unity?").
    - Start with a 3-minute mission story (e.g., before Chapter 2).
    - For small groups, combine exercises (e.g., Covenant Writing and Calling Reflection, Chapter 1).
    - ⏱ Optional: Skip reflections (e.g., Trust Reflection, Chapter 3) if pressed.
    - **Materials:** As above, plus sample agendas (Chapter 4).

- **Four 3-Hour Retreats (12 hours):**
  - **Structure:**
    - Retreat 1: Chapters 1–2 (2 sessions, 3 hours).
    - Retreat 2: Chapters 3–4 (2 sessions, 3 hours).
    - Retreat 3: Chapters 5–6 (2 sessions, 3 hours).
    - Retreat 4: Chapters 7–8 (2 sessions, 3 hours).
  - **Timing:** Monthly or biweekly (e.g., 6:00 PM–9:00 PM, 15-minute break).
  - **Use Case:** Fits boards with regular meetings for gradual integration.
  - **Facilitation Tips:**
    - Use 60 to 90-minute sessions for each chapter.
    - Select 3 questions and 2 exercises per chapter (e.g., Mission Audit and Purpose Reflection, Chapter 2).
    - Share outputs in Effective Church Leadership Community forum (Appendix, page 76, e.g., "Post Chapter 5's Financial Dashboard").
    - Use Zoom whiteboard for hybrid mapping (e.g., Budget Alignment Map, Chapter 6).
    - For large groups, assign roles (e.g., scribe for Conflict Map, Chapter 7).
    - ⏱ Optional: Skip grids (e.g., Say No Discernment Grid, Chapter 6) if time is short.
    - **Materials:** Budget copies (Chapter 6), prayer templates (Chapter 8).

- **Eight 1–1.5 Hour Sessions (8–12 hours):**
    - **Structure:** One chapter per session (Chapters 1–4, 5–8).
    - **Timing:** Weekly (e.g., 7:00 PM–8:30 PM, 60–90 minutes).
    - **Use Case:** Matches Effective Church Leadership Community's eight-week training for structured learning.
    - **Facilitation Tips:**
        - Use 60 to 90-minute sessions for each chapter.
        - Post Effective Church Leadership Community reflections (Appendix, page 67, e.g., "Share a discernment practice from Chapter 4").
        - For hybrid, use Zoom polls (e.g., "What protects our mission?" in Chapter 11).
        - For small groups, focus on discussion (e.g., 2 questions in Chapter 8).
        - ⏱ Optional: Skip journals (e.g., Courage Journal, Chapter 8) if pressed.
        - **Materials:** As above, tailored per session.

Anniversary Retreat: Sustaining the Vision (3–4 hours)

Together, we renew governance through the Anniversary Retreat, using Chapters 9–12 (pages 51–63) to sustain leadership vitality. Homework: *Embracing Our Call* Chapters 5, 9, 13, 16 (2 hours, with summaries in Appendix, page 67).

- **Session 1: Chapter 9 – Sustaining Leadership (60–90 minutes):**
    - **Focus:** Prevents fatigue through rest and support.
    - **Activities:** Burnout Audit, Self-Care Plan. Discuss "What sustains our board's vitality?"
    - **Homework:** *Embracing Our Call* Chapter 5 (~15 minutes).
    - **Webinar:** Preventing Leadership Burnout (Appendix, page 76).
    - **Facilitation Tips:**
        - Use Burnout Worksheet from Effective Church Leadership Community, page 76.
        - Start with "What sustains us?"
        - For hybrid, share plans via Zoom chat.
        - Post in Effective Church Leadership Community: "Share a self-care strategy" (Appendix, page 76).
        - **Materials:** Burnout Worksheet, paper, pens.
- **Session 2: Chapter 10 – Governance as Covenant (60–90 minutes):**
    - **Focus:** Renews commitments for unity.
    - **Activities:** Covenant Design, Role Review. Discuss "What fosters our board's covenantal unity?"
    - **Homework:** *Embracing Our Call* Chapter 9 (~15 minutes).
    - **Webinar:** Duties of Corporate Officers (Appendix, page 67).
    - **Facilitation Tips:**
        - Use Covenant Template from Effective Church Leadership Community, page 76.
        - Start with "What strengthens our covenant?"
        - Post covenants in Effective Church Leadership Community (Appendix, page 76).
        - **Materials:** Covenant Template, role list.
- **Session 3: Chapter 11 – Transparency, Accountability, and Trust (60–90 minutes):**
    - **Focus:** Strengthens accountability for trust.
    - **Activities:** Transparency Inventory, Trust Mapping. Discuss "What trust-building system protects our mission?"
    - **Homework:** *Embracing Our Call* Chapter 13 (~15 minutes).
    - **Webinar:** Creating a Healthy Church Governance Culture (Appendix, page 76).
    - **Facilitation Tips:**
        - Use Transparency Inventory Template from Effective Church Leadership Community, page 76.
        - For hybrid, use Zoom whiteboard.
        - Post trust maps in Effective Church Leadership Community (Appendix, page 67).
        - **Materials:** Transparency Inventory Template, flipchart, markers.
- **Session 4: Chapter 12 – Mentoring New Leaders (60–90 minutes):**

- - -
    - **Focus:** Prepares future leaders for continuity.
    - **Activities:** Mentorship Map. Discuss "How do we entrust leadership with grace?"
    - **Homework:** *Embracing Our Call* Chapter 16 (~15 minutes).
    - **Webinar:** Leadership Transitions (Appendix, page 76).
    - **Facilitation Tips:**
        - Pair leaders/mentees.
        - Post maps in Effective Church Leadership Community (Appendix, page 76).
        - **Materials:** Mentorship Map Template, paper, pens.
- **Timing:** One day (e.g., 9:00 AM–1:00 PM, 15-minute breaks).
- **Use Case:** Annual renewal for governance milestones.
- **Facilitation Tips:**
    - Select 2 questions, 1 exercise per session.
    - Begin with a 2-minute prayer or story of renewal.
    - For hybrid, use Zoom breakout rooms (e.g., Self-Care Plan, Chapter 9).
    - Post in Effective Church Leadership Community (Appendix, page 76, e.g., "How does Chapter 11's trust-building system protect our mission?").
    - ⏱ Optional: Skip reflections (e.g., Unity Reflection, Chapter 10) if time is short.
    - **Materials:** Burnout Worksheet, Covenant Template, Transparency Inventory Template, Mentorship Map Template, role list, flipchart, markers, pens.
    - End with a prayer for renewal to unify the retreat.

Quick Start Guide

Together, we lead faithfully using *Serving the Call*.

- **Session Start:** Begin each session with a 2-minute prayer or silence to center on God's presence.
- **Content Selection:** Select 2 Group Reflection Questions (e.g., "What stood out?" or "How do we align with our Calling?" in Chapter 1) and 1 Group Practice Exercise (e.g., Covenant Writing, Chapter 1) for 60–90-minute sessions.
- **Homework Check:** Confirm participants read *Embracing Our Call* homework (1 hour, or read brief summaries in Appendix, page 72). Use prompts like "What resonated from *Embracing Our Call*?" to connect homework.
- **Materials Prep:** Provide Materials (e.g., mission statements for Chapter 2's Mission Audit, Covenant Template from Effective Church Leadership Community, page 76).
- **Hybrid Sessions:** Use Zoom breakout rooms (e.g., Role Clarity, Chapter 3) or polls (e.g., "What protects our mission?" in Chapter 11).
- **Effective Church Leadership Community Engagement:** Post reflections in Effective Church Leadership Community forums (Appendix, page 73, e.g., "Share a mission insight from Chapter 2").
- **Time Management:** ⏱ Optional: Skip secondary exercises (e.g., Mission Moment, Chapter 1) if time is tight.
- **Planning Tool:** Use the Session Planner Template (page 13) to organize sessions, and download templates (e.g., Financial Dashboard, Chapter 5) from Effective Church Leadership Community, page 76.
- **Closing Reflection:** End with: "Where did we sense God's presence?" For the Anniversary Retreat, ask: "How does Chapter 11's trust-building system sustain our mission?"

FAQ

- **What if we're short on time?** ⏱ Select 1 question and 1 exercise (e.g., Mission Audit, Chapter 2) for 60-minute sessions.
- **How do we manage hybrid formats?** Use Zoom chat for reflections (e.g., Calling insights, Chapter 1) and whiteboard for exercises (e.g., Budget Alignment Map, Chapter 6).
- **What about large groups?** Divide into pairs for exercises (e.g., Conflict Map, Chapter 7). Assign a scribe.
- **What if we lack Effective Church Leadership Community access?** Use Appendix summaries (page 70) for webinars or contact service@ChurchTrainingCenter.com for templates.
- **How can we go deeper?** Use Anniversary Retreat or Effective Church Leadership Community chapters (9, 10, 11, 12, page 76).
- **How do we handle sensitive topics?** Set ground rules for conflict discussions (Chapter 7, e.g., "Listen without interrupting").
- **What if participants miss homework?** Summarize *Embracing Our Call* chapters (e.g., "Chapter 1 emphasizes spiritual governance", ~2 minutes).

Using This Workbook in Effective Church Leadership Community

Together, we grow through Effective Church Leadership Community's platform.

- **Forum Posts:** Post session reflections in forums (Appendix, page 72, e.g., "How did Chapter 2's Mission Audit shape your mission?").
- **File Sharing:** Share outputs (e.g., Covenant Design, Chapter 10; Budget Alignment Map, Chapter 6) via file uploads.
- **Webinar Discussions:** Discuss webinars asynchronously (e.g., "How did 'Good Governance' inform Chapter 1's Calling?").
- **Support:** Ensure Effective Church Leadership Community supports uploads and forums.

Facilitator's Preparation Checklist

This checklist consolidates Materials, preparation steps, and Effective Church Leadership Community prompts for all retreats, streamlining facilitation. Download templates from the Effective Church Leadership Community (page 76) or contact service@ChurchTrainingCenter.com.

- **Retreat 1: Building the Foundation (4–5 hours, pages 13–30):**
    - **Materials:** Paper, pens, mission statements (Chapter 2), Mission Audit Template (Chapter 2), Covenant Template (Chapter 3), role list (Chapter 3), flipchart (Chapter 4), markers (Chapter 4), Meeting Agenda Template (Chapter 4).
    - **Prep Steps:** Confirm *Embracing Our Call* Chapters 1–3, 10 read (1 hour) or use Appendix summaries (page 72). Prepare Zoom breakout rooms for hybrid (e.g., Mission Audit, Chapter 2). Select 2 questions, 1 exercise per chapter (e.g., Covenant Writing, Chapter 3). Plan 60–90-minute sessions for each chapter.
    - **Effective Church Leadership Community Prompts (Appendix, page 73):** Share a Calling insight (Chapter 1), mission insight (Chapter 2), trust practice (Chapter 3), discernment practice (Chapter 4).
- **Retreat 2: Strengthening the Call (4–5 hours, pages 31–48):**
    - **Materials:** Sample financial report (Chapter 5), Financial Dashboard Template (Chapter 5), budget copies (Chapter 6), Budget Alignment Map Template (Chapter 6), ministry statements (Chapter 6), flipchart (Chapter 7), markers (Chapter 7), Conflict Map Template (Chapter 7), decision list (Chapter 8), Commissioning Prayer Template (Chapter 8).
    - **Prep Steps:** Confirm *Embracing Our Call* Chapters 4, 15, 23, 27 read (1 hour) or use Appendix summaries (page 70). Prepare Zoom whiteboard for hybrid (e.g., Budget Alignment Map, Chapter 6). Select 2 questions, 1 exercise per chapter (e.g., Conflict Map, Chapter 7). Plan 60–90-minute sessions for each chapter.
    - **Effective Church Leadership Community Prompts (Appendix, page 73):** Share a dashboard idea (Chapter 5), budget alignment (Chapter 6), conflict resolution step (Chapter 7), commissioning prayer (Chapter 8).
- **Anniversary Retreat: Sustaining the Vision (3–4 hours, pages 49–66):**
    - **Materials:** Burnout Worksheet (Chapter 9), Covenant Template (Chapter 10), role list (Chapter 10), Transparency Inventory Template (Chapter 11), flipchart (Chapter 11), markers (Chapter 11), Mentorship Map Template (Chapter 12).

- - **Prep Steps:** Confirm *Embracing Our Call* Chapters 5, 9, 13, 16 read (1 hour) or use Appendix summaries (page 72). Prepare Zoom breakout rooms for hybrid (e.g., Mentorship Map, Chapter 12). Select 2 questions, 1 exercise per chapter (e.g., Transparency Inventory, Chapter 11). Plan 60–90-minute sessions for each chapter.
  - **Effective Church Leadership Community Prompts (Appendix, page 73):** Share a self-care strategy (Chapter 9), covenant commitment (Chapter 10), transparency practice (Chapter 11), mentoring idea (Chapter 12).
- **General Prep:**
  - Test Effective Church Leadership Community forum access for uploads.
  - Prepare prayer prompts (e.g., "Guide us, Spirit," Chapter 1).
  - Ensure Zoom setup for hybrid sessions (breakout rooms, whiteboard, polls).
  - Review Facilitator's Guide for format-specific tips.

Session Planner Template

Field	Details
Chapter	
Reflection Question(s)	
Exercise	
Materials	
Time Allotted	
EFFECTIVE CHURCH LEADERSHIP COMMUNITY Prompt (Appendix, page 73)	
Notes	

Retreat 1: Building the Foundation

And when you turn to the right or to the left, your ears will hear a voice behind you, saying, 'This is the way; walk in it.'

— Isaiah 30:21

Retreat 1 lays the cornerstone for faithful governance, equipping new board members to align with God's calling through mission discernment, clear roles, and purposeful meetings. Over 4–5 hours, Chapters 1–4 guide you to respond to the Spirit's invitation, clarify your church's purpose, build trust through stewardship, and transform meetings into sacred spaces. Prepare with *Embracing Our Call* readings (1 hour, with brief summaries in Appendix, page 72). Together, we share insights in EFFECTIVE CHURCH LEADERSHIP COMMUNITY forums, ensuring governance matches other trainings' scope while rooting leadership in spiritual clarity and unity. See the Retreat-at-a-Glance (page 3) and Facilitator's Guide (page 5) for planning.

Retreat Facilitation Overview: Plan 4–5 hours, using 60-minute sessions for Chapters 1 and 3, 75-minute sessions for Chapters 2 and 4. Start with a 2-minute prayer or mission story to center on God's presence. Use Zoom breakout rooms for exercises like Mission Audit (Chapter 2) or Covenant Writing (Chapter 3). Post outputs in EFFECTIVE CHURCH LEADERSHIP COMMUNITY forums (e.g., "Share a mission insight," Appendix, page 73). Download templates from the Effective Church Leadership Community (page 76) and use the Session Planner Template (page 13) for planning.

Chapter 1: Serving Our Call

Governance as spiritual practice

📖 Then I heard the voice of the Lord saying, 'Whom shall I send, and who will go for us?' And I said, 'Here am I; send me!'

— Isaiah 6:8

📖 Reading Assignment

Read *Embracing Our Call* Chapter 1: The Spirit Has Placed Us Here before this session (~15 minutes). This chapter frames governance as a sacred response to God's call, unifying mission, effort, and assets. It prepares you to see board service as purposeful stewardship.

💬 Scriptural Reflection

Isaiah's bold response, "Here am I; send me!" captures the heart of church governance as a divine invitation to serve God's mission. Leadership is not a task assigned by chance but a sacred call to stewardship. This scripture invites humility to listen, prayer to discern, and trust in the Spirit's guidance. As board members, you weave together your community's gifts to reflect God's glory. Isaiah's willingness challenges us to see governance as a holy commitment, saying "yes" to God's work through your church.

🎓 Teaching Content

Three Pillars of Governance
Church governance is a spiritual practice, unifying mission, effort, and assets through three pillars: Calling (responding to God's invitation), Energy (directing prayerful effort), and Resources (using time, talent, and treasure purposefully). These pillars guide boards to lead with purpose, not reaction. For example, a board opened meetings with a discernment question: "Where is God moving in our community?" This shifted focus from tasks to faith, fostering unity.

Learning from Examples
Another board prayed over budget cuts, discerning outreach priorities, which strengthened trust. A third invited a congregant to share a mission story—how a food pantry transformed a family—grounding decisions in God's work. When conflicts arise, Spirit-led boards pause, pray, and seek wisdom, turning tension into discernment. Purposeful discernment prevents reactive decisions, ensuring mission, effort, and assets serve the church's calling, helping it flourish, not merely function.

🔑 Key Takeaways

- Governance unifies mission, effort, and assets with God's calling.
- Board service is purposeful stewardship, rooted in prayer.
- The Spirit guides decisions through communal discernment.

💭 Group Reflection Questions

- How do you personally feel called to serve on the church board?
- Where have you seen the Spirit's presence in our governance work?
- What aspects of board service feel most spiritual to you?
- How can we ensure our work remains grounded in God's call?
- What practices help us discern God's direction as a board?

✻ Group Practice Exercises

1. Covenant Writing (10 minutes): In small groups, draft a board covenant, naming commitments to faithful service (e.g., "We will begin with prayer"). Share one commitment.
2. Calling Reflection (5 minutes): Journal on "What calls me to serve on this board?" Share one insight with a partner.
3. Mission Moment (3 minutes): Invite a member to share a 3-minute story of God's work (e.g., a ministry's impact). ⏱ *Optional*: Skip if time is tight.

🎥 Webinar Reference

Good Governance
Read brief summary, Appendix, page 70. Available in the Effective Church Leadership Community. [Summary: Introduces spiritual governance, unifying mission, effort, and assets for purpose-driven leadership.]

✍ Facilitator Notes [Guided/Self-Guided]

- **Homework**:
    - Confirm *Embracing Our Call* Chapter 1 read (1 hour).
    - If unread: Use Appendix summary, page 73 (~1–2 minutes).
    - Summarize: "Chapter 1 frames governance as a sacred call."
- **Session**:
    - Select 2 questions (e.g., 1, 4) and 1 exercise (e.g., Covenant Writing) for 60 minutes.
    - Start: 2-minute prayer, "Guide us, Spirit, to serve your call."
    - Prompt: "How did Chapter 1's focus on unifying mission, effort, and assets inspire us?"
    - Post: See Appendix, page 73, for EFFECTIVE CHURCH LEADERSHIP COMMUNITY forum prompts (e.g., "Share a Calling insight").
- **Hybrid**: Use Zoom breakout rooms for Covenant Writing; for large groups, share one covenant aloud.
- **Templates**: Download Covenant Template from the Effective Church Leadership Community, pages 76.
- **Time-Saving**: ⏱ *Optional*: Skip Mission Moment if pressed.
- **Materials**: Paper, pens, Covenant Template.

Chapter 2: Finding Our Purpose

Discerning God's unique call

For surely I know the plans I have for you, says the Lord, plans for your welfare and not for harm, to give you a future with hope.

— Jeremiah 29:11

Reading Assignment

Read *Embracing Our Call* Chapter 2: Paths Made Straight before this session (~15 minutes). This chapter explores discerning God's call through prayerful listening, aligning efforts with purpose. It prepares you to clarify your church's mission.

Scriptural Reflection

God's promise to Jeremiah offers hope and purpose amid uncertainty, assuring plans for a future rooted in divine care. Church governance mirrors this promise, seeking God's unique call for your community through prayerful listening rather than reactive strategies. The board's role is to discern the Spirit's whisper—perhaps a call to compassion, justice, or witness—and guide the church toward it. Jeremiah's assurance invites boards to trust that God's plans unfold when we pause, pray, and align our efforts, ensuring governance reflects divine direction.

Teaching Content

Discerning God's Call

Every church has a unique purpose, but boards often react to crises—declining attendance, budget shortfalls—rather than discern God's call. Prayer, community conversations, and scripture help boards hear the Spirit's voice, often as compassion, justice, or witness. For example, a church facing membership decline asked, "Who is our neighbor now?" Their discernment led to a new outreach ministry, growing faithfulness over numbers.

Practical Discernment Tools

Another board held retreats to discern youth needs, launching vibrant programs that re-engaged families. A third invited congregants to share stories—like a tutoring program's impact—grounding decisions in mission. Clarity in purpose fosters unity and shared responsibility, avoiding drift from past practices. Boards act as midwives, guiding the church's next faithful step through communal listening, ensuring effort and assets align with God's call.

Key Takeaways

- Purpose is communal, shaped by collective discernment.
- Governance listens to the Spirit before leading.
- Boards clarify mission to unify the church's purpose.

Group Reflection Questions

- How would you describe our church's purpose in one sentence?
- When did we last ask, "What is God asking of us now?"
- What practices help us listen for the Spirit's guidance?
- What distractions pull us from our shared purpose?
- How can we prioritize discernment in our meetings?

🛠 Group Practice Exercises

1. Mission Audit (12 minutes): In small groups, analyze the church's mission statement against ministries. Identify one alignment and one gap; share findings.
2. Purpose Reflection (5 minutes): Journal on "What is our church's unique purpose?" Share one insight.
3. Community Story-Sharing (3 minutes): Invite a member to share a 3-minute story of God's work (e.g., outreach impact). ⏱ *Optional*: Skip if pressed.

🎥 Webinar Reference

Mission, Vision & Values
See brief summary, Appendix, page 70. Available in the Effective Church Leadership Community.
[Summary: Guides leaders in defining mission, vision, values to align with God's calling.]

✍ Facilitator Notes [Guided/Self-Guided]

- **Homework**:
    - Confirm *Embracing Our Call* Chapter 2 read (1 hour).
    - If unread: Use Appendix summary, page 72 (~1–2 minutes).
    - Summarize: "Chapter 2 emphasizes discerning purpose."
- **Session**:
    - Select 2 questions (e.g., 1, 3) and 1 exercise (e.g., Mission Audit) for 75 minutes.
    - Start: 2-minute silence, "Spirit, reveal our purpose."
    - Prompt: "How did Chapter 2's listening focus shape our mission?"
    - Post: See Appendix, page 73, for EFFECTIVE CHURCH LEADERSHIP COMMUNITY forum prompts (e.g., "Share a mission insight").
- **Hybrid**: Share audit gaps via Zoom chat; for large groups, divide for auditing.
- **Templates**: Download Mission Audit Template from the Effective Church Leadership Community, page 76.
- **Time-Saving**: ⏱ *Optional*: Skip Community Story-Sharing if pressed.
- **Materials**: Mission statement copies, Mission Audit Template, paper, pens.

Chapter 3: Leadership as Sacred Trust

Building trust in governance

📖

Like good stewards of the manifold grace of God, serve one another with whatever gift each of you has received.

— 1 Peter 4:10

📖 Reading Assignment

Read *Embracing Our Call* Chapter 3: The Threefold Cord before this session (~15 minutes). This chapter explores spiritual, relational, and organizational alignment for trust. It prepares you to steward gifts with integrity.

💭 Scriptural Reflection

Peter's call to stewardship frames leadership as a sacred trust, where each member's gifts are offered to God's mission. Governance is not about power but humbly stewarding God's grace. This scripture challenges boards to lead with integrity, building trust through transparency and accountability. By serving with diverse gifts—listening, planning, praying—boards create a culture where trust flourishes, uniting the church in its purpose to serve faithfully.

🎓 Teaching Content

Foundations of Trust
Trust is the bedrock of governance, enabling boards to steward God's mission with integrity. Transparency in financial reporting, accountability in decisions, and discernment in conflicts build this trust. For example, a board recovering from a scandal shared monthly budget reports, inviting questions to rebuild confidence. Another resolved a worship style dispute through listening sessions, grounding decisions in scripture (Colossians 3:14).

Practical Trust-Building
A third board clarified roles to boost volunteer engagement, ensuring clear expectations. Clarity in roles and processes fosters shared responsibility, preventing mistrust from secrecy. Regular prayer unifies boards, as when one prayed together to resolve a staffing issue. Purposeful stewardship prevents hasty decisions, ensuring gifts are used faithfully to advance the church's mission, not personal agendas.

🔑 Key Takeaways

- Trust grows through transparency and accountable service.
- Governance stewards God's gifts with humility.
- Prayerful discernment builds board and congregational unity.

💬 Group Reflection Questions

- What practices build trust within our board?
- How do we model transparency to the congregation?
- When have we seen trust strengthen our governance?
- What steps can deepen our board's integrity?
- How can we address trust breakdowns faithfully?

✹ Group Practice Exercises

1. Leadership Covenant (12 minutes): In small groups, draft a covenant for trust (e.g., "We will share decisions openly"). Share one commitment.
2. Trust Reflection (5 minutes): Journal on "What builds trust in our board?" Share one insight.
3. Role Clarity Exercise (5 minutes): List board roles; clarify one ambiguity (e.g., budget approval). ⏱ *Optional*: Skip if pressed.

🎥 Webinar Reference

Creating a Healthy Church Governance Culture
Read brief summary, Appendix, page 70. Available in the Effective Church Leadership Community.
[Summary: Encourages transparency, accountability, trust in leadership.]

Facilitator Notes [Guided/Self-Guided]

- **Homework**:
    - Confirm *Embracing Our Call* Chapter 3 read (1 hour).
    - If unread: Use Appendix summary, page 72 (~1–2 minutes).
    - Summarize: "Chapter 3 emphasizes trust through alignment."
- **Session**:
    - Select 2 questions (e.g., 1, 4) and 1 exercise (e.g., Leadership Covenant) for 60 minutes.
    - Start: 2-minute prayer, "God, unite us in trust."
    - Prompt: "How did Chapter 3's alignment build trust?"
    - Post: See Appendix, page 73, for EFFECTIVE CHURCH LEADERSHIP COMMUNITY forum prompts (e.g., "Share a trust practice").
- **Hybrid**: Use Zoom breakout rooms for covenant drafting; for large groups, pair for Role Clarity.
- **Templates**: Download Covenant Template from the Effective Church Leadership Community, page 76.
- **Time-Saving**: *Optional*: Skip Trust Reflection if pressed.
- **Materials**: Covenant Template, role list, paper, pens.

Chapter 4: Meetings as Sacred Space

Creating space for discernment

For where two or three are gathered in my name, I am there among them.

— Matthew 18:20

Reading Assignment

Read *Embracing Our Call* Chapter 10: Meeting in the Presence of God before this session (~15 minutes). This chapter explores spiritual practices for meetings, ensuring discernment. It prepares you to transform meetings into sacred spaces.

Scriptural Reflection

Jesus' promise of presence transforms meetings into sacred spaces where the Spirit dwells. Governance meetings are opportunities to discern God's call together, not just complete tasks. This scripture invites boards to approach meetings with reverence, balancing practicality with prayer. By gathering in Jesus' name, boards create space for the Spirit to guide decisions, resolve conflicts, and unify the church, ensuring meetings reflect God's purpose.

Teaching Content

Sacred Meeting Practices
Effective meetings blend spiritual depth with practical outcomes, creating spaces for discernment. Begin with prayer or 2-minute silence to center on the Spirit, followed by mission stories to ground discussions. For example, a board facing budget disputes used 5-minute discernment pauses before votes, fostering unity. Another prioritized a congregant's story about a youth ministry, aligning decisions with purpose.

Avoiding Common Traps
Active listening—paraphrasing others' views—reduces conflicts, as when a board resolved a scheduling dispute by hearing all sides. Clarity in agendas prevents rushed decisions; one board delayed a staffing vote to pray, uncovering a better solution. Structured agendas (prayer, reports, discernment, closing) ensure reflection time. Purposeful practices transform meetings from draining tasks to sacred spaces, advancing God's call with unity.

Key Takeaways

- Meetings are sacred when centered on God's presence.
- Discernment transforms routine governance into spiritual work.
- Structured, prayerful meetings unify the church's purpose.

Group Reflection Questions

- Do our meetings feel sacred, routine, or draining?
- What practices invite God's presence into our meetings?
- When have we sensed the Spirit guiding discussions?
- How can we create more space for discernment?
- What distractions pull us from a spiritual focus?

✹ Group Practice Exercises

1. Meeting Mapping (10 minutes): In small groups, map a recent meeting's flow (e.g., prayer, agenda). Identify one improvement (e.g., discernment pause).
2. Sacred Space Reflection (5 minutes): Journal on "What makes a meeting sacred?" Share one insight.
3. Agenda Redesign (5 minutes): Draft a new agenda with prayer and reflection; share one change. ⏱ *Optional*: Skip if pressed.

🎥 Webinar Reference

Leading Effective Church Meetings
See brief summary, Appendix, page 70. Available in the Effective Church Leadership Community.
[Summary: Structures meetings for meaningful, purpose-driven discussions.]

👍 Facilitator Notes [Guided/Self-Guided]

- **Homework**:
    - Confirm *Embracing Our Call* Chapter 10 read (1 hour).
    - If unread: Use Appendix summary, page 72 (~1–2 minutes).
    - Summarize: "Chapter 10 emphasizes spiritual meetings."
- **Session**:
    - Select 2 questions (e.g., 1, 4) and 1 exercise (e.g., Agenda Redesign) for 75 minutes.
    - Start: 2-minute silence, "Jesus, be present among us."
    - Prompt: "How did Chapter 10's practices inspire our meetings?"
    - Post: See Appendix, page 73, for EFFECTIVE CHURCH LEADERSHIP COMMUNITY forum prompts (e.g., "Share a discernment practice").
- **Hybrid**: Use Zoom whiteboard for Meeting Mapping; for large groups, divide for agenda drafting.
- **Templates**: Download Meeting Agenda Template from the Effective Church Leadership Community, page 76.
- **Time-Saving**: ⏱ *Optional*: Skip Sacred Space Reflection if pressed.
- **Materials**: Flipchart, markers, Meeting Agenda Template, paper, pens.

Retreat 2: Strengthening the Call

There is one body and one Spirit, just as you were called to the one hope of your calling… one Lord, one faith, one baptism, one God and Father of all, who is above all and through all and in all.

— Ephesians 4:4–6

Retreat 2 deepens your board's governance, forming faithful leaders to steward resources, resolve conflicts with compassion, and commission with boldness. Over 4–5 hours, Chapters 8, 9, 14, and 17 guide new members to unify finances with purpose, lead through challenges with faith, and send leaders into service with courage. Building on Retreat 1's foundation, this retreat equips you with advanced skills, surpassing standard trainings. Prepare with *Embracing Our Call* readings (1 hour, with brief summaries in Appendix, page 47). Together, we share insights in EFFECTIVE CHURCH LEADERSHIP COMMUNITY forums, strengthening your church's mission. See the Retreat-at-a-Glance (page 3) and Facilitator's Guide (page 5) for planning.

Retreat Facilitation Overview: Plan 4–5 hours, using 75-minute sessions for Chapters 8 and 9, 60-minute sessions for Chapters 14 and 17. Start with a 2-minute prayer or mission story to center on God's presence. Use Zoom whiteboard for exercises like Budget Alignment Map (Chapter 9) or Conflict Map (Chapter 14). Post outputs in EFFECTIVE CHURCH LEADERSHIP COMMUNITY forums (Appendix, page 47). Download templates from the Effective Church Leadership Community (pages 48–49) and use the Session Planner Template (page 8) for planning.

Chapter 5: Making Sense of the Numbers

Financial clarity as stewardship

📖

Whoever is faithful in a very little is faithful also in much…

— Luke 16:10

Reading Assignment

Read *Embracing Our Call* Chapter 4: Stewarding the Storehouse before this session (~15 minutes). This chapter explores stewardship of time, talent, and treasure, emphasizing faithful management. It prepares you for clear financial oversight.

Scriptural Reflection

Jesus' teaching on faithfulness in small matters underscores financial stewardship as a sacred trust. Governance requires clarity in managing resources, not for control, but to honor God's provision. Luke 16:10 challenges boards to approach budgets and reports with diligence, reflecting integrity in every detail. Purposeful stewardship builds trust, ensuring resources serve the church's calling. By being faithful in "little" financial tasks—clear reports, honest audits—boards invite the congregation to join in God's mission with confidence and unity.

Teaching Content

Stewarding Resources
Financial clarity is essential for governance, enabling boards to steward resources with trust and purpose. Understanding budgets, reports, and policies empowers leaders to unify finances with purpose. For example, a board struggling with opaque reports created a simplified financial dashboard, shared monthly, boosting congregational trust. Another board, new to finance, held a workshop with their treasurer to learn terms like "designated funds," improving decisions.

Building Trust Through Clarity
Regular audits, even in small churches, foster accountability; one board caught a bookkeeping error through an audit, correcting it openly. Clarity in communication—using stories like how a youth program grew—connects numbers to ministry. Thoughtful education, such as pairing novices with "finance buddies," prevents mistrust from jargon or secrecy. These practices ensure resources are faithful tools, not burdens, strengthening the church's mission with integrity.

Key Takeaways

- Financial clarity is a spiritual act of stewardship.
- Transparent reporting builds congregational trust.
- Education empowers boards for purpose-aligned oversight.

Group Reflection Questions

- What does financial stewardship mean to our board?
- How transparent are our financial processes with the congregation?
- When have we felt confident in our budget or reports?
- What financial terms or processes need clarification?
- How can we unify finances with our church's purpose?

✸ Group Practice Exercises

1. Dashboard Draft (10 minutes): In small groups, sketch a one-page financial dashboard summarizing key metrics (e.g., income, expenses). Share one feature.
2. Financial Reflection (5 minutes): Journal on "What makes financial stewardship faithful?" Share one insight.
3. Finance Buddy (5 minutes): Pair to explain one financial term (e.g., "endowment"). Discuss clarity gained. ⏱ *Optional*: Skip if pressed.

🎥 Webinar Reference

Building Financial Literacy Among Church Leaders
Read brief summary, Appendix, page 70. Available in the Effective Church Leadership Community.
[Summary: Builds financial management skills, ensuring clarity and trust.]

📖 Facilitator Notes [Guided/Self-Guided]

- **Homework**:
    - Confirm *Embracing Our Call* Chapter 4 read (1 hour).
    - If unread: Use Appendix summary, page 72 (~1–2 minutes).
    - Summarize: "Chapter 4 frames stewardship as honoring God's gifts."
- **Session**:
    - Select 2 questions (e.g., 1, 4) and 1 exercise (e.g., Dashboard Draft) for 75 minutes.
    - Start: 2-minute prayer, "God, guide our stewardship."
    - Prompt: "How did Chapter 4's stewardship focus shape our clarity?"
    - Post: See Appendix, page 73, for EFFECTIVE CHURCH LEADERSHIP COMMUNITY forum prompts (e.g., "Share a dashboard idea").
- **Hybrid**: Use Zoom whiteboard for Dashboard Draft; for large groups, divide for drafting.
- **Templates**: Download Financial Dashboard Template from the Effective Church Leadership Community, pages 76.
- **Time-Saving**: ⏱ *Optional*: Skip Finance Buddy if pressed.
- **Materials**: Sample financial report, Financial Dashboard Template, paper, pens.

Chapter 6: Faithful Stewardship of Church Resources

Aligning financial decisions with God's purpose

Each of you must give as you have made up your mind, not reluctantly or under compulsion, for God loves a cheerful giver.

— 2 Corinthians 9:7

📖 Reading Assignment

Read *Embracing Our Call* Chapter 15: Accountability in Action before this session (~15 minutes). This chapter explores transparent budgeting to unify resources with purpose. It prepares you for joyful, mission-driven stewardship.

💬 Scriptural Reflection

Paul's call to cheerful giving reflects the heart of financial stewardship: decisions rooted in joy and purpose, not obligation. Governance unifies resources with God's call, ensuring budgets serve mission, not habit. This scripture challenges boards to approach finances with prayerful discernment, trusting God's abundance. By giving freely—time, talent, treasure—boards model generosity, inviting the congregation to invest in God's work. Joyful stewardship transforms budgets into testimonies of mission, uniting the church in shared purpose.

🎓 Teaching Content

Budgets as Mission

Budgets are more than numbers; they embody the church's purpose, balancing mission with financial health. Joyful stewardship aligns spending with God's call through prayerful review and congregational input. For example, a board mapped their budget to ministries, redirecting funds from outdated programs to a growing outreach, sparking revival. Another held visioning sessions with members, funding a community center that embodied their call.

Avoiding Common Pitfalls

Regular budget reviews—quarterly or mid-year—ensure alignment; one board cut a non-essential expense after prayer, freeing funds for mission. Clarity in priorities prevents habitual spending, as when a board used mission-matching grids to evaluate expenses. Transparent communication, like sharing budget stories (e.g., a scholarship-funded youth retreat), fosters trust. These practices ensure resources are cheerful offerings, advancing God's work with joy and unity.

🔑 Key Takeaways

- Budgets prioritize mission through joyful giving.
- Prayerful discernment unifies resources with purpose.
- Transparent budgeting unites the church in stewardship.

💭 Group Reflection Questions

- Where is our budget unified with our church's purpose?
- How do we discern financial priorities as a board?
- When have we seen God's abundance in our giving?
- What expenses could we prayerfully decline?
- How can we involve the congregation in budgeting?

🛠 Group Practice Exercises

1. Budget Alignment Map (12 minutes): In small groups, map one budget category (e.g., outreach) to the church's mission. Identify one alignment or gap; share findings.
2. Ministry Mission Match (5 minutes): Journal on "Which ministry best reflects our purpose?" Share one example.
3. Say No Discernment Grid (5 minutes): List one expense to decline; discuss why it misaligns with mission. ⏱ *Optional*: Skip if pressed.

📽 Webinar Reference

Budgeting for Church Programs
See brief summary, Appendix, page 70. Available in the Effective Church Leadership Community.
[Summary: Allocates funds to programs while maintaining financial health.]

⚑ Facilitator Notes [Guided/Self-Guided]

- **Homework**:
    - Confirm *Embracing Our Call* Chapter 15 read (1 hour).
    - If unread: Use Appendix summary, page 72 (~1–2 minutes).
    - Summarize: "Chapter 15 emphasizes transparent budgeting."
- **Session**:
    - Select 2 questions (e.g., 1, 4) and 1 exercise (e.g., Budget Alignment Map) for 75 minutes.
    - Start: 2-minute prayer, "Spirit, unify our resources."
    - Prompt: "How did Chapter 15's accountability inspire budgeting?"
    - Post: See Appendix, page 73, for EFFECTIVE CHURCH LEADERSHIP COMMUNITY forum prompts (e.g., "Share a budget alignment").
- **Hybrid**: Share maps via Zoom chat; for large groups, divide for mapping.
- **Templates**: Download Budget Alignment Map Template from the Effective Church Leadership Community, page 76.
- **Time-Saving**: ⏱ *Optional*: Skip Say No Grid if pressed.
- **Materials**: Budget copies, Budget Alignment Map Template, ministry statements, paper, pens.

Chapter 7: Courage, Compassion, and Commitment

Leading through difficulty with faith and love

📖

So do not fear, for I am with you; do not be dismayed, for I am your God...

— Isaiah 41:10

📖 Reading Assignment

Read *Embracing Our Call* Chapter 23: Blessed Are the Peacemakers before this session (~15 minutes). This chapter explores governance's role in fostering unity through conflict. It prepares you to lead with compassion and courage.

💭 Scriptural Reflection

Isaiah's assurance of God's presence offers courage for leading through conflict. Governance during difficulties requires compassion to hear all voices, commitment to stay engaged, and faith to trust God's guidance. This scripture reminds boards that challenges are opportunities to model love, not failures. By leading with courage—naming tensions—and compassion—listening deeply—boards transform conflicts into growth, ensuring the church remains united in its purpose, with God as their strength.

🎓 Teaching Content

Navigating Conflict Faithfully
Conflict is inevitable, but courageous, compassionate leadership turns challenges into opportunities. Commitment means staying present, not avoiding tension. For example, a board facing worship style disputes used 5-minute spiritual pauses before discussions, fostering unity. Another trained in conflict resolution, using listening circles to resolve a staffing issue, rebuilding trust.

Practical Tools for Unity
Naming tensions early prevents escalation; one board ignored a volunteer dispute, causing disengagement, but later held mediated talks, restoring relationships. Clarity in conflict resolution—using tools like conflict maps or spiritual pause plans—centers discussions. Purposeful discernment prevents reactive decisions, as when a board prayed over a budget cut, finding a compromise. These practices ensure conflicts strengthen the church's mission, reflecting God's presence in difficulty.

🔑 Key Takeaways

- Courage names conflict with faith and openness.
- Compassion fosters unity through loving listening.
- Commitment sustains leadership, strengthening purpose.

💬 Group Reflection Questions

- How do we respond to conflict with faith and courage?
- When has compassion resolved a challenge in our church?
- What gives us strength to stay committed in difficulties?
- How can we foster unity during board conflicts?
- What practices discern God's guidance in tension?

🛠 Group Practice Exercises

1. Conflict Map (10 minutes): In small groups, map a recent conflict (e.g., parties, issues). Identify one resolution step; share it.
2. Spiritual Pause Plan (5 minutes): Journal on "How can we pause during conflicts?" Share one practice.
3. Discernment Partner Circle (5 minutes): Pair to practice listening to a conflict perspective; summarize partner's view. ⏱ *Optional*: Skip if pressed.

🎥 Webinar Reference

Church Conflict Resolution
Read brief summary, Appendix, page 70. Available in the Effective Church Leadership Community.
[Summary: Guides leaders in managing conflicts to foster unity and trust.]

✍ Facilitator Notes [Guided/Self-Guided]

- **Homework**:
    - Confirm *Embracing Our Call* Chapter 23 read (1 hour).
    - If unread: Use Appendix summary, page 72 (~1–2 minutes).
    - Summarize: "Chapter 23 emphasizes peacemaking."
- **Session**:
    - Select 2 questions (e.g., 1, 4) and 1 exercise (e.g., Conflict Map) for 60 minutes.
    - Start: 2-minute silence, "God, grant us courage."
    - Prompt: "How did Chapter 23's peacemaking inspire unity?"
    - Post: See Appendix, page 73, for EFFECTIVE CHURCH LEADERSHIP COMMUNITY forum prompts (e.g., "Share a conflict resolution step").
- **Hybrid**: Use Zoom whiteboard for Conflict Map; for large groups, pair for Discernment Circle.
- **Templates**: Download Conflict Map Template from the Effective Church Leadership Community, page 76.
- **Time-Saving**: ⏱ *Optional*: Skip Spiritual Pause Plan if pressed.
- **Materials**: Flipchart, markers, Conflict Map Template, paper, pens.

Chapter 8: A Benediction of Boldness

Blessing and sending with courage and faith

📖

Be strong and courageous. Do not be afraid… for the Lord your God will be with you wherever you go.

— Joshua 1:9

📖 Reading Assignment

Read *Embracing Our Call* Chapter 27: Unity in Calling before this session (~15 minutes). This chapter explores commissioning leaders in unity for God's purpose. It prepares you to bless transitions with boldness.

💭 Scriptural Reflection

Joshua's charge to be strong and courageous frames governance endings as bold beginnings. Boards conclude their work by commissioning leaders to carry God's call forward, trusting in divine presence. This scripture invites boards to bless their service with courage, releasing fears and embracing faith. By ending with a benediction—prayer, gratitude, or ritual—boards unify the church, sending leaders into mission with confidence. Governance is about preparing the church to go where God leads, together.

📣 Teaching Content

Commissioning for Mission
The end of a governance cycle is a commissioning, blessing the church's purpose with boldness. Boards reflect on their season, release burdens, and send leaders forward in faith. For example, a board wrote prayers on their building's walls during a renovation, blessing future ministries. Another prayed over their budget, commissioning staff to lead boldly.

Faithful Transitions
Public blessings, like a congregational service honoring board service, unify the church; one board held such a service, boosting engagement. Clarity in transitions—using debriefs to name God's work or prayers to bless new leaders—ensures continuity. Purposeful discernment prevents abrupt endings; one board delayed a vote to pray, ensuring a faithful handoff. These practices make endings courageous beginnings, rooted in God's promise, strengthening the church for its next steps.

🔑 Key Takeaways

- Commissioning renews leadership for God's purpose.
- Bold endings unify the church through blessing.
- Faithful transitions reflect trust in God's presence.

💬 Group Reflection Questions

- What has God unfolded in our church this season?
- Where have we seen boldness in our governance?
- What do we need to release as this cycle ends?
- How can we commission new leaders faithfully?
- How do we honor our service as sacred?

✜ Group Practice Exercises

1. Seasonal Debrief (10 minutes): In small groups, list one success and one challenge from this season. Share one lesson learned.
2. Commissioning Prayer (5 minutes): Draft a group prayer to bless new leaders; read it aloud.
3. Courage Journal (5 minutes): Journal on "What bold step will I take?" Share one commitment. ⏱ *Optional*: Skip if pressed.

🎥 Webinar Reference

Why Be Do
Read brief summary, Appendix, page 70. Available in the Effective Church Leadership Community.
[Summary: Inspires leaders to align actions with God's calling, commissioning bold service.]

📖 Facilitator Notes [Guided/Self-Guided]

- **Homework**:
  - Confirm *Embracing Our Call* Chapter 27 read (1 hour).
  - If unread: Use Appendix summary, page 72 (~1–2 minutes).
  - Summarize: "Chapter 27 emphasizes commissioning in unity."
- **Session**:
  - Select 2 questions (e.g., 1, 4) and 1 exercise (e.g., Commissioning Prayer) for 60 minutes.
  - Start: 2-minute prayer, "God, make us bold."
  - Prompt: "How did Chapter 27's unity inspire commissioning?"
  - Post: See Appendix, page 73, for EFFECTIVE CHURCH LEADERSHIP COMMUNITY forum prompts (e.g., "Share a commissioning prayer").
- **Hybrid**: Share prayers via Zoom chat; for large groups, pair for Courage Journal.
- **Templates**: Download Commissioning Prayer Template from the Effective Church Leadership Community, page 76.
- **Time-Saving**: ⏱ *Optional*: Skip Courage Journal if pressed.
- **Materials**: Decision list, Commissioning Prayer Template, paper, pens.

Anniversary Retreat: Sustaining the Vision

Write the vision; make it plain on tablets, so that a runner may read it.

— Habakkuk 2:2

The Anniversary Retreat renews your board's governance, forming faithful leaders for sacred responsibility through enduring leadership, covenantal unity, transparency, and mentoring. Over 3–4 hours, Chapters 5, 7, 11, and 12 guide new members to prevent burnout, recommit to shared purpose, build trust through accountability, and prepare future leaders. Building on Retreats 1 and 2, this retreat ensures long-term vitality, surpassing standard trainings. Prepare with *Embracing Our Call* readings (1 hour, with brief summaries in Appendix, page 72). Together, we share insights in EFFECTIVE CHURCH LEADERSHIP COMMUNITY forums, sustaining your church's mission. See the Retreat-at-a-Glance (page 3) and Facilitator's Guide (page 4) for planning.

Retreat Facilitation Overview: Plan 3–4 hours, using 60-minute sessions for each Chapter. Start with a 2-minute prayer or renewal story to center on God's presence. Use Zoom breakout rooms for exercises like Mentorship Map (Chapter 12) or Transparency Inventory (Chapter 11). Post outputs in EFFECTIVE CHURCH LEADERSHIP COMMUNITY forums (Appendix, page 73). Download templates from the Effective Church Leadership Community (page 76) and use the Session Planner Template (page 13) for planning.

Chapter 9: Sustaining Leadership

Preventing burnout in governance

📖

When Moses' hands grew tired, they took a stone and put it under him and he sat on it. Aaron and Hur held his hands up—one on one side, one on the other—so that his hands remained steady till sunset

— Exodus 17:12

📖 Reading Assignment

Read *Embracing Our Call* Chapter 5: Until the Sun Set before this session (~15 minutes). This chapter explores enduring leadership through shared support and rest. It prepares you to prevent burnout with resilience.

💭 Scriptural Reflection

The image of Aaron and Hur supporting Moses' weary hands reveals the power of shared leadership. Governance can exhaust even the faithful, but God provides strength through community and rest. Exodus 17:12 challenges boards to recognize limits as invitations to rely on others and the Spirit. Enduring leadership requires courage to name fatigue, wisdom to share burdens, and faith to rest, ensuring boards remain steady in their calling to serve faithfully.

🎯 Teaching Content

Preventing Burnout
Leadership burnout—marked by fatigue, disengagement, or resentment—threatens governance, but intentional practices sustain vitality. Boards must name signs of strain, like overcommitted members or skipped meetings, and act proactively. For example, a board noticing burnout rotated roles yearly, refreshing energy. Another created a self-care plan, scheduling retreats and prayer breaks, boosting resilience.

Shared Support and Rest
Sharing burdens, as Aaron and Hur did, is key; one board paired seasoned and new members, easing pressure on veterans. Regular audits of time commitments foster clarity, as when a small church cut redundant meetings, freeing time for mission. Thoughtful rest—Sabbath practices or delegation—renews faith, preventing turnover seen when a board lost members to unchecked stress. These practices ensure governance remains a joyful calling, sustaining the church's mission.

🔑 Key Takeaways

- Shared support prevents burnout in leadership.
- Time audits foster enduring governance practices.
- Sabbath and delegation renew boards' vitality.

💬 Group Reflection Questions

- Where do we see signs of fatigue in our board's work?
- How can we share leadership burdens more effectively?
- When have we felt renewed in our governance service?
- What rest practices could sustain our board's vitality?
- How can we discern when to pause or delegate tasks?

🛠 Group Practice Exercises

1. Burnout Audit (12 minutes): In small groups, list board tasks and time commitments. Identify one overextension; propose a solution (e.g., delegate).
2. Self-Care Plan (5 minutes): Journal on "What renews me in service?" Share one practice.
3. Support Circle (5 minutes): Pair to discuss "What support do I need?" Summarize partner's need. ⏱ *Optional*: Skip if pressed.

🎥 Webinar Reference

Preventing Leadership Burnout
Read brief summary, Appendix, page 70. Available in the Effective Church Leadership Community.
[Summary: Identifies and addresses burnout for enduring leadership.]

🏠 Facilitator Notes [Guided/Self-Guided]

- **Homework:**
    - Confirm *Embracing Our Call* Chapter 5 read (1 hour).
    - If unread: Use Appendix summary, page 72 (~1–2 minutes).
    - Summarize: "Chapter 5 emphasizes shared support for leadership."
- **Session:**
    - Select 2 questions (e.g., 1, 4) and 1 exercise (e.g., Burnout Audit) for 60 minutes.
    - Start: 2-minute prayer, "God, sustain us in service."
    - Prompt: "How did Chapter 5's support model inspire resilience?"
    - Post: See Appendix, page 73, for EFFECTIVE CHURCH LEADERSHIP COMMUNITY forum prompts (e.g., "Share a self-care strategy").
- **Hybrid:** Use Zoom polls for audit solutions; for large groups, divide for auditing.
- **Templates:** Download Burnout Worksheet from the Effective Church Leadership Community, page 76.
- **Time-Saving:** ⏱ *Optional:* Skip Support Circle if pressed.
- **Materials:** Burnout Worksheet, paper, pens.

Chapter 10: Governance as Covenant

Building a covenantal culture

Because of all this we make a firm agreement in writing…

— Nehemiah 9:38

Reading Assignment

Read *Embracing Our Call* Chapter 9: Sealed in Covenant before this session (~15 minutes). This chapter explores covenantal governance for unity and commitment. It prepares you to foster a shared agreement.

Scriptural Reflection

Nehemiah's covenant, sealed in writing, reflects a community's commitment to God's purpose. Governance as covenant binds boards in shared promises, fostering unity beyond tasks. This scripture challenges boards to lead with intentional agreements, grounding decisions in faith. A covenantal culture prioritizes relationships, accountability, and discernment, ensuring the church's mission endures. By making firm agreements, boards model God's faithfulness, inviting the congregation to live as a covenant people, united in their purpose.

Teaching Content

Covenantal Governance
Governance thrives when boards operate as a covenant community, bound by shared commitments to God's call. Covenants—written or spoken—clarify roles, expectations, and values, reducing conflict. For example, a board facing role disputes drafted a covenant promising open communication, resolving tensions. Another reviewed roles annually, ensuring clarity; when a treasurer overstepped, the covenant guided correction.

Strengthening Unity
Spiritual practices, like starting meetings with prayer, unify boards, as one did to align diverse views. Clarity in expectations fosters shared responsibility, preventing confusion from vague roles. Regular covenant renewals, like Nehemiah's agreement, recommit boards; one held an annual recommitment service, boosting morale. These practices build a culture where trust and purpose flourish, ensuring governance reflects God's faithfulness for the long term.

Key Takeaways

- Covenants foster unity through shared commitments.
- Clear roles strengthen board culture and trust.
- Renewals recommit boards to God's purpose.

Group Reflection Questions

- What makes our board feel like a covenant community?
- How clear are our roles and expectations as a board?
- When have we felt unified in our governance work?
- What covenant practices could deepen our commitment?
- How can we renew our covenant annually with faith?

🛠 Group Practice Exercises

1. Covenant Design (12 minutes): In small groups, draft a board covenant (e.g., "We will pray before decisions"). Share one commitment.
2. Role Review (5 minutes): List one unclear board role; propose a clarification (e.g., "Define treasurer's duties").
3. Unity Reflection (5 minutes): Journal on "What unifies our board?" Share one insight. ⏱ *Optional*: Skip if pressed.

🎥 Webinar Reference

Duties of Corporate Officers
Read brief summary, Appendix, page 70. Available in the Effective Church Leadership Community.
[Summary: Clarifies officer roles for effective, covenantal governance.]

✍ Facilitator Notes [Guided/Self-Guided]

- **Homework**:
    - Confirm *Embracing Our Call* Chapter 9 read (1 hour).
    - If unread: Use Appendix summary, page 72 (~1–2 minutes).
    - Summarize: "Chapter 9 emphasizes covenantal unity."
- **Session**:
    - Select 2 questions (e.g., 1, 4) and 1 exercise (e.g., Covenant Design) for 60 minutes.
    - Start: 2-minute prayer, "God, bind us in covenant."
    - Prompt: "How did Chapter 9's covenant inspire unity?"
    - Post: See Appendix, page 73, for EFFECTIVE CHURCH LEADERSHIP COMMUNITY forum prompts (e.g., "Share a covenant commitment").
- **Hybrid**: Share covenants via Zoom chat; for large groups, pair for Role Review.
- **Templates**: Download Covenant Template from the Effective Church Leadership Community, page 76.
- **Time-Saving**: ⏱ *Optional*: Skip Unity Reflection if pressed.
- **Materials**: Covenant Template, role list, paper, pens.

Chapter 11: Transparency, Accountability, and Trust

Fostering credibility through trust-building systems

📖

Examine everything carefully; hold fast to what is good...

— 1 Thessalonians 5:21

Reading Assignment

Read *Embracing Our Call* Chapter 13: Protected by Purpose before this session (~15 minutes). This chapter explores transparency and accountability to protect mission. It prepares you to build trust through systems.

Scriptural Reflection

Paul's call to examine everything carefully urges boards to govern with transparency and accountability, ensuring trust. Governance is not blind trust but discerning stewardship, holding fast to what aligns with God's purpose. This scripture challenges boards to create trust-building systems—audits, reports, policies—that foster credibility. Transparent practices invite congregational trust, while accountability protects the mission. By examining carefully, boards build a culture where faith and integrity unite, sustaining the church's calling.

Teaching Content

Building Trust
Transparency and accountability are pillars of trust, requiring consistent practices like clear financial reports, open decision-making, and regular audits. For example, a board regained trust post-misconduct by publishing quarterly reports and hosting Q&A sessions. Another created a transparency inventory, listing decision processes (e.g., budget approvals), clarifying governance.

Practical Tools
Trust-building systems share responsibility; one board used trust mapping to assign roles, preventing overreliance on one member. Clarity in systems prevents secrecy, as when a board's closed-door decisions sparked distrust, resolved through open forums. Regular reviews—financial, policy, or roles—ensure integrity; a small church's annual audit caught errors, reinforcing trust. These practices, grounded in discernment, make governance credible, inviting congregational support for God's mission.

Key Takeaways

- Transparency builds trust through clear reporting.
- Trust-building systems protect the church's mission.
- Consistent practices foster integrity and credibility.

Group Reflection Questions

- How transparent are our board's decisions to the congregation?
- Where do trust-building systems strengthen our governance?
- When have we felt trust grow through our practices?
- What transparency practice could we adopt or improve?
- How can we ensure accountability without control?

🛠 Group Practice Exercises

1. Transparency Inventory (10 minutes): In small groups, list one decision process (e.g., budget approval). Clarify how it's shared; propose one improvement.
2. Trust Mapping (5 minutes): Map board roles and responsibilities; identify one gap (e.g., unclear auditor).
3. Integrity Reflection (5 minutes): Journal on "What builds trust in our board?" Share one practice. ⏱ *Optional:* Skip if pressed.

🎥 Webinar Reference

Creating a Healthy Church Governance Culture
Read brief summary, Appendix, page 70. Available in the Effective Church Leadership Community.
[Summary: Encourages transparency, accountability, and trust in leadership.]

✍ Facilitator Notes [Guided/Self-Guided]

- **Homework**:
    - Confirm *Embracing Our Call* Chapter 13 read (1 hour).
    - If unread: Use Appendix summary, page 72 (~1–2 minutes).
    - Summarize: "Chapter 13 emphasizes transparency for mission."
- **Session**:
    - Select 2 questions (e.g., 1, 4) and 1 exercise (e.g., Transparency Inventory) for 60 minutes.
    - Start: 2-minute prayer, "God, guide our integrity."
    - Prompt: "How did Chapter 13's transparency inspire trust?"
    - Post: See Appendix, page 73, for EFFECTIVE CHURCH LEADERSHIP COMMUNITY forum prompts (e.g., "Share a transparency practice").
- **Hybrid**: Use Zoom whiteboard for Trust Mapping; for large groups, divide for inventory.
- **Templates**: Download Transparency Inventory Template from the Effective Church Leadership Community, page 76.
- **Time-Saving**: ⏱ *Optional*: Skip Integrity Reflection if pressed.
- **Materials**: Transparency Inventory Template, flipchart, markers, paper, pens.

Chapter 12: Mentoring New Leaders

Preparing the next generation for governance

📖

You then, my child, be strong in the grace that is in Christ Jesus; and what you have heard from me… entrust to faithful people who will be able to teach others as well.

— 2 Timothy 2:1–2

Reading Assignment

Read *Embracing Our Call* Chapter 16: Subjecting to Governing Authorities before this session (~15 minutes). This chapter explores mentoring for leadership transitions, ensuring continuity. It prepares you to entrust leadership with grace.

Scriptural Reflection

Paul's charge to Timothy to entrust teachings to faithful others underscores mentoring as a sacred task. Governance endures when boards prepare new leaders, passing on wisdom and grace. This scripture challenges boards to strengthen the next generation through encouragement and trust in Christ's grace, not control. Mentoring builds a legacy, ensuring the church's mission thrives beyond one board's tenure. By entrusting leadership, boards reflect God's faithfulness, sustaining the church for future callings.

Teaching Content

Mentoring for Continuity
Mentoring new leaders ensures governance continuity, preparing the next generation for God's call. Boards must identify and nurture potential leaders proactively. For example, a board created a mentorship program, pairing veterans with newcomers, doubling volunteer engagement. Another invited young members to shadow meetings, sparking interest; one mentee later became chair.

Building Confidence
Mentorship maps pair strengths (e.g., a planner with a visionary), as one board did to balance roles. Clarity in mentoring prevents gaps; a board's failure to mentor caused a leadership void, resolved through emergency training. Regular mentoring—workshops, co-leading, or prayer partnerships—builds confidence. One board held quarterly "leadership lunches," fostering relationships. These practices ensure new leaders are equipped, sustaining the church's purpose with grace and strength.

Key Takeaways

- Mentoring prepares leaders for sustainable governance.
- Intentional programs build confidence and continuity.
- Entrusting leadership reflects faith in God's purpose.

Group Reflection Questions

- Who mentored you into leadership, and how did it shape you?
- How are we identifying potential leaders in our church?
- What mentoring practices could we adopt for new leaders?
- Where do we see God calling the next generation?
- How can we entrust leadership with grace and strength?

🛠 Group Practice Exercises

1. Mentorship Map (12 minutes): In small groups, map current leaders to potential mentees based on strengths. Propose one pairing; share it.
2. Legacy Reflection (5 minutes): Journal on "What wisdom should we pass on?" Share one insight.
3. Mentoring Plan (5 minutes): Draft one mentoring activity (e.g., shadowing); discuss feasibility. ⏱ *Optional:* Skip if pressed.

🎥 Webinar Reference

Leadership Transitions: Succession Planning for Church Leaders
Read brief summary, Appendix, page 70. Available in the Effective Church Leadership Community.
[Summary: Guides boards in mentoring and transitioning leaders for continuity.]

🕮 Facilitator Notes [Guided/Self-Guided]

- **Homework**:
    - Confirm *Embracing Our Call* Chapter 16 read (1 hour).
    - If unread: Use Appendix summary, page 72 (~1–2 minutes).
    - Summarize: "Chapter 16 emphasizes mentoring for continuity."
- **Session**:
    - Select 2 questions (e.g., 1, 4) and 1 exercise (e.g., Mentorship Map) for 60 minutes.
    - Start: 2-minute prayer, "Christ, strengthen our mentoring."
    - Prompt: "How did Chapter 16's transitions inspire mentoring?"
    - Post: See Appendix, page 76, for EFFECTIVE CHURCH LEADERSHIP COMMUNITY forum prompts (e.g., "Share a mentoring idea").
- **Hybrid**: Share maps via Zoom chat; for large groups, pair for Mentoring Plan.
- **Templates**: Download Mentorship Map Template from the Effective Church Leadership Community, page 76.
- **Time-Saving**: ⏱ *Optional*: Skip Mentoring Plan if pressed.
- **Materials**: Mentorship Map Template, paper, pens.

Appendix:
Webinar Summaries and Supplemental Resources

Together, we enhance *Serving the Call: Forming Faithful Leaders for Sacred Responsibility* with this Appendix, providing webinar summaries, supplemental chapter references, and resources to support new governance body members. Brief summaries (~100 words, ~1–2 minutes to read) offer key insights for participants opting not to watch the ~1-hour webinars, ensuring accessible preparation.

⏱ *Optional*: Use summaries instead of webinars to save time, as noted in the Facilitator's Guide (page 4). Resources, including EFFECTIVE CHURCH LEADERSHIP COMMUNITY forum prompts and templates, streamline exercises. Use with the Retreat-at-a-Glance (page 1) and Session Planner Template (page 13) to sustain your church's mission.

Webinar Summaries

1. **Good Governance (Chapter 1, Retreat 1, page 17)**
   Brief summary (~100 words, ~1–2 minutes): Introduces spiritual governance, framing board service as a sacred response to God's call. It explores unifying mission, effort, and assets for purpose-driven leadership, using examples like prayerful budget decisions. Tools include discernment questions (e.g., "Where is God moving?") and covenant drafting. Transparency and prayer unify boards, avoiding reactive governance. Ideal for new members, it complements Chapter 1's focus on governance as a spiritual practice, equipping boards to steward faithfully.

2. **Mission, Vision & Values (Chapter 2, Retreat 1, page 21)**
   Brief summary (~100 words, ~1–2 minutes): Guides leaders in defining mission, vision, and values to align with God's calling. Tools like mission audits assess ministry alignment, while story-sharing grounds decisions. Examples include churches redefining outreach through discernment. Prayerful listening ensures clarity in purpose, surpassing strategic planning. It supports Chapter 2's discernment focus, offering steps to unify congregations around a shared vision, vital for new board members.

3. **Creating a Healthy Church Governance Culture (Chapters 3, 11, Retreat 1, page 25; Anniversary Retreat, page 61)**
   Brief summary (~100 words, ~1–2 minutes): Fosters transparency, accountability, and trust, essential for board unity. Strategies include open financial reporting and listening sessions to build confidence. Examples show boards resolving disputes with transparency inventories. Spiritual practices like prayer sustain healthy culture. It supports Chapter 3's trust-building and Chapter 11's accountability focus, equipping new leaders with tools to ensure governance reflects integrity and faith.

4. **Leading Effective Church Meetings (Chapter 4, Retreat 1, page 29)**
   Brief summary (~100 words, ~1–2 minutes): Structures meetings for purpose-driven discussions, blending spirituality and practicality. Tools like discernment pauses and clear agendas foster unity. Examples include boards using mission stories to align decisions. Starting with prayer and active listening avoids rushed outcomes, supporting Chapter 4's focus on sacred spaces. It equips facilitators to balance efficiency and discernment, advancing God's call.

5. **Building Financial Literacy Among Church Leaders (Chapter 5, Retreat 2, page 35)**
   Brief summary (~100 words, ~1–2 minutes): Builds financial management skills, ensuring clarity and trust in stewardship. It covers budgets, reports, and audits, offering tools like financial dashboards. Examples show boards simplifying reports to engage congregations. Transparency is framed as spiritual stewardship, supporting Chapter 5's clarity focus. It empowers new leaders to understand terms like "designated funds," unifying decisions with purpose.

6. **Budgeting for Church Programs (Chapter 6, Retreat 2, page 39)**
   Brief summary (~100 words, ~1–2 minutes): Guides boards in allocating funds to programs while maintaining financial health, prioritizing mission. Tools like budget alignment maps link spending to purpose. Examples include boards redirecting funds to outreach through discernment. Joyful giving and transparent communication support Chapter 6's stewardship focus, equipping leaders to balance ministry and sustainability for God's call.

7. **Church Conflict Resolution (Chapter 7, Retreat 2, page 43)**
   Brief summary (~100 words, ~1–2 minutes): Equips leaders to manage conflicts with

courage and compassion, fostering unity. Tools like conflict maps and spiritual pauses transform challenges. Examples show boards resolving disputes through listening circles. Prayerful discernment avoids reactive decisions, supporting Chapter 7's focus on leading through difficulty. It ensures conflicts strengthen mission, vital for new leaders.

8. **Why Be Do (Chapter 8, Retreat 2, page 47)**
   Brief summary (~100 words, ~1–2 minutes): Inspires leaders to align actions with God's calling, framing endings as bold commissionings. Tools like commissioning prayers and debriefs bless transitions. Examples include boards holding blessing services to unify congregations. Courage and faith support Chapter 8's focus on bold leadership, equipping boards to send leaders with strength.

9. **Preventing Leadership Burnout (Chapter 9, Anniversary Retreat, page 53)**
   Brief summary (~100 words, ~1–2 minutes): Identifies and addresses burnout, promoting enduring leadership through rest and support. Tools like burnout audits and self-care plans renew boards. Examples show boards rotating roles to refresh energy. Shared responsibility supports Chapter 9's focus on sustaining leadership, ensuring new leaders maintain vitality for long-term mission.

10. **Duties of Corporate Officers (Chapter 10, Anniversary Retreat, page 57)**
    Brief summary (~100 words, ~1–2 minutes): Clarifies officer roles (e.g., chair, treasurer) for covenantal governance. Tools like role reviews and covenants unify boards. Examples show boards resolving disputes through clear expectations. Spiritual practices like prayer support Chapter 10's covenant focus, equipping new officers to lead with integrity and purpose.

11. **Leadership Transitions: Succession Planning for Church Leaders (Chapter 12, Anniversary Retreat, page 65)**
    Brief summary (~100 words, ~1–2 minutes): Guides boards in mentoring and transitioning leaders for continuity. Tools like mentorship maps prepare new leaders. Examples show boards pairing veterans with newcomers to build confidence. Entrusting leadership with grace supports Chapter 12's mentoring focus, ensuring governance endures for new members.

12. **Building Strong Governance Structures in the Church (Supplemental)**
    Brief summary (~100 words, ~1–2 minutes): Outlines board and committee structures to support mission. Tools like bylaws reviews and role assignments enhance efficiency. Examples show churches streamlining committees. Alignment with purpose complements *Serving the Call*'s core chapters, ideal for new boards seeking structural clarity. Available in the Effective Church Leadership Community, page 76.

13. **Church Compliance with State and Federal Regulations (Supplemental)**
    Brief summary (~100 words, ~1–2 minutes): Navigates legal requirements, including tax-exempt status, with tools like compliance checklists to ensure adherence. Examples show boards avoiding penalties through audits. Stewardship through legal integrity complements *Serving the Call*'s accountability focus, supporting new leaders in compliance. Available in the Effective Church Leadership Community, page 76.

14. **The Role of Governance in Church Growth (Supplemental)**
    Brief summary (~100 words, ~1–2 minutes): Explores governance's role in sustainable growth through mission alignment. Tools like visioning sessions engage congregations. Examples show boards launching ministries through discernment. It supports *Serving the Call*'s mission focus, ideal for growth-oriented new boards. Available in the Effective Church Leadership Community, page 76.

15. **Best Practices for Financial Reporting in Churches (Supplemental)**
    Brief summary (~100 words, ~1–2 minutes): Details transparent financial reporting to build

trust. Tools like report templates simplify communication. Examples show boards boosting engagement through clear budgets. It enhances *Serving the Call*'s stewardship chapters, supporting new leaders in accountability. Available in the Effective Church Leadership Community, page 76.

16. **Creating a Culture of Generosity in Your Church (Supplemental)**
Brief summary (~100 words, ~1–2 minutes): Offers steps to increase giving through stewardship campaigns. Tools like story-based appeals inspire generosity. Examples show churches funding missions through engagement. It complements *Serving the Call*'s budgeting focus, encouraging joyful giving for new leaders. Available in the Effective Church Leadership Community, page 76.

17. **Volunteer Management: Recruiting, Retaining, and Motivating Volunteers (Supplemental)**
Brief summary (~100 words, ~1–2 minutes): Builds a strong volunteer base through recruitment and retention strategies. Tools like volunteer audits match skills. Examples show churches boosting participation through mentoring. It supports *Serving the Call*'s leadership focus, ensuring mission vitality for new boards. Available in the Effective Church Leadership Community, page 76.

Supplemental Chapter References

The following *Serving the Call* chapters, available in the Effective Church Leadership Community (page 76), deepen governance training for new board members. Each complements the core 12 chapters (1–12) and *Embracing Our Call*'s spiritual focus, accessible via the Community's table of contents.

- **Chapter 13: Movement Leads to Stillness (~590 words):**
Explores balancing action and reflection, using discernment pauses to sustain mission focus. It enhances Retreat 1's meeting practices (Chapter 4, page 29), ideal for boards seeking deeper spiritual practices. Available in the Effective Church Leadership Community, page 76.
- **Chapter 14: Protected by Purpose (~590 words):**
Details safeguarding mission through policies and trust-building systems, with tools like transparency inventories. It strengthens Anniversary Retreat's accountability focus (Chapter 11, page 61), supporting new leaders in trust-building. Available in the Effective Church Leadership Community, page 76.
- **Chapter 15: Plans Committed in Prayer (~590 words):**
Guides prayerful financial planning to unify budgets with mission, using mission-matching grids. It complements Retreat 2's stewardship (Chapter 6, page 39), equipping new leaders for budgeting. Available in the Effective Church Leadership Community, page 76.
- **Chapter 16: Written on Our Hearts (~590 words):**
Emphasizes documenting governance practices for continuity, with tools like role documentation. It supports Anniversary Retreat's mentoring (Chapter 12, page 65), ensuring transitions for new leaders. Available in the Effective Church Leadership Community, page 76.

Supplemental Resources

Effective Church Leadership Community Forum Prompts

The following prompts, used in Facilitator Notes (Chapters 1–12), encourage reflection in the Effective Church Leadership Community forums to deepen governance training. Post outputs after each session to foster community learning.

Chapter	Prompt
1: Serving Our Call	Share a Calling insight from Chapter 1's reflection or Covenant Writing exercise.
2: Finding Our Purpose	Share a mission insight from Chapter 2's Mission Audit or Purpose Reflection.
3: Leadership as Sacred Trust	Share a trust practice from Chapter 3's Leadership Covenant or Role Clarity exercise.
4: Meetings as Sacred Space	Share a discernment practice from Chapter 4's Meeting Mapping or Agenda Redesign.
5: Making Sense of the Numbers	Share a dashboard idea from Chapter 5's Dashboard Draft or Financial Reflection.
6: Faithful Stewardship of Church Resources	Share a budget alignment from Chapter 6's Budget Alignment Map or Ministry Mission Match.
7: Courage, Compassion, and Commitment	Share a conflict resolution step from Chapter 7's Conflict Map or Spiritual Pause Plan.
8: A Benediction of Boldness	Share a commissioning prayer from Chapter 8's Seasonal Debrief or Commissioning Prayer.
9: Sustaining Leadership	Share a self-care strategy from Chapter 9's Burnout Audit or Self-Care Plan.
10: Governance as Covenant	Share a covenant commitment from Chapter 10's Covenant Design or Role Review.
11: Transparency, Accountability, and Trust	Share a transparency practice from Chapter 11's Transparency Inventory or Trust Mapping.
12: Mentoring New Leaders	Share a mentoring idea from Chapter 12's Mentorship Map or Legacy Reflection.

Template Descriptions

These templates, downloadable from the Effective Church Leadership Community (page 76), support *Serving the Call* exercises, streamlining facilitation for new board members. Customize these tools to enhance governance practices, as outlined in the Facilitator's Guide (page 4). For template access without Effective Church Leadership Community, contact service@ChurchTrainingCenter.com.

- **Leadership Covenant Template (Chapter 3, Retreat 1, page 25):**
  A Word document (~100 words) for drafting board covenants, with prompts for

commitments (e.g., "We will pray before decisions"). Supports Chapter 3's trust-building exercise, fostering unity. Access at the Effective Church Leadership Community, page 76.

- **Meeting Agenda Template (Chapter 4, Retreat 1, page 29):**
A Word document (~50 words) for structuring mission-driven meetings, with sections for prayer, reports, and discernment. Supports Chapter 4's agenda redesign exercise, ensuring sacred spaces. Access at the Effective Church Leadership Community, page 76.

- **Mission Audit Template (Chapter 2, Retreat 1, page 21):**
A Word document (~50 words) for analyzing mission statement alignment with ministries. Supports Chapter 2's mission audit exercise, clarifying purpose. Access at the Effective Church Leadership Community, page 76.

- **Financial Dashboard Template (Chapter 5, Retreat 2, page 35):**
An Excel spreadsheet (~50 cells) for summarizing financial metrics (e.g., income, expenses). Supports Chapter 5's dashboard draft exercise, promoting clarity. Access at the Effective Church Leadership Community, page 76.

- **Budget Alignment Map Template (Chapter 6, Retreat 2, page 39):**
A Word document (~50 words) for mapping budget categories to mission priorities. Supports Chapter 6's budget alignment exercise, ensuring stewardship. Access at the Effective Church Leadership Community, page 76.

- **Conflict Map Template (Chapter 7, Retreat 2, page 43):**
A Word document (~50 words) for mapping conflicts to identify resolution steps. Supports Chapter 7's conflict map exercise, fostering unity. Access at the Effective Church Leadership Community, page 76.

- **Commissioning Prayer Template (Chapter 8, Retreat 2, page 47):**
A Word document (~50 words) for drafting prayers to bless new leaders. Supports Chapter 8's commissioning prayer exercise, ensuring bold transitions. Access at the Effective Church Leadership Community, page 76.

- **Burnout Worksheet (Chapter 9, Anniversary Retreat, page 53):**
A Word document (~50 words) for auditing board tasks and time commitments. Supports Chapter 9's burnout audit exercise, promoting sustainability. Access at the Effective Church Leadership Community, page 76.

- **Transparency Inventory Template (Chapter 11, Anniversary Retreat, page 61):**
A Word document (~50 words) for listing decision processes to ensure transparency. Supports Chapter 11's transparency inventory exercise, building trust. Access at the Effective Church Leadership Community, page 76.

- **Mentorship Map Template (Chapter 12, Anniversary Retreat, page 65):**
A Word document (~50 words) for mapping leaders to mentees based on strengths. Supports Chapter 12's mentorship map exercise, ensuring continuity. Access at the Effective Church Leadership Community, page 76.

Effective Church Leadership Community

Equipping Leaders to Serve Faithfully, Lead Boldly, and Follow the Spirit Together

Leadership in the church is sacred, courageous work. You don't have to do it alone. The Effective Church Leadership Community is a free online space for pastors, treasurers, board members, and ministry leaders to connect, grow, and lead with clarity. Through webinars, tools, best practices, and supportive conversation, we help churches align energy and resources with God's calling—not alone, but together. Whether you're stepping into leadership or guiding others, this community offers practical wisdom and spiritual encouragement for the road ahead.

We bring together pastors, treasurers, board members, and ministry leaders in pursuit of fulfilling God's calling — not alone, but together.

Why Join?

This free online community helps local church leaders:

☩ Align energy and resources with God's calling

💬 Connect with peers for support and collaboration

✖ Access best practices in governance and finance

🎓 Grow through webinars, trainings, and book studies

📚 Explore a growing library of policies and tools

👐 Lead with greater confidence and faith

📖 *"Without guidance, a people falls; but victory is won through many counselors."*

— *Proverbs 11:14*

✦ Scan to Join for Free

Use your phone's camera or visit the link below:

Scan to join or visit:
https://community.churchtrainingcenter.com/plans/1529909

Let's Keep Going

If this book has sparked clarity, raised questions, or left you longing for more support, we're here to help. Church Training Center offers coaching, training, and consulting for church boards, pastors, and leaders who want to align faithfully with God's call—and sustain the journey over time. To explore next steps or schedule a consultation, visit:
www.ChurchTrainingCenter.com

Or reach out directly at: service@ChurchTrainingCenter.com

Glossary of Governance & Finance Terms

Bylaws: The church's official governing rules that define leadership structures, voting, meetings, and procedural guidelines.

Calling: The unique purpose or direction God is asking a church to follow in a specific season.

Covenant: A shared agreement among board members to guide behavior and decision-making, fostering unity (e.g., Chapter 7's shared agreement).

Designated Funds: Contributions given for a specific purpose, by donor request, honored by board agreement.

Discernment: A spiritual process of listening for God's guidance, especially in decision-making, often through prayer and group reflection.

Endowment: A long-term fund held by a church, where the principal is invested and earnings may be used for ministry.

Fiduciary Responsibility: The legal and ethical obligation of board members to act in the best interest of the organization and its mission.

GAAP: 'Generally Accepted Accounting Principles,' a standardized framework for financial reporting and transparency.

Restricted Funds: Contributions with legal obligations for their use, based on donor instructions that must be followed.

Undesignated Funds: Contributions made without a specific purpose, available for use at the board's discretion.

10 Practices of Spirit-Led Governance

1. Begin each retreat or session with prayer to center on God's presence.

2. Align decisions with the church's discerned purpose, not just past practices.

3. Use financial dashboards and budgets to reflect ministry stories (Chapters 8–9).

4. Incorporate discernment pauses in meetings to listen for the Spirit (Chapter 4).

5. Clarify board roles to prevent burnout and ensure accountability (Chapter 7).

6. Foster trust through transparent reporting and open communication (Chapter 11).

7. Address conflicts early with courage and compassion (Chapter 14).

8. Mentor new leaders to sustain governance continuity (Chapter 12).

9. Revisit covenants annually to renew commitment (Chapter 7).

10. End sessions by naming where God's guidance was sensed, reinforcing spiritual focus.

Scripture Index

REATREAT 1: BUILDING THE FOUNDATION
Isaiah 30:31

Chapter 1: Serving Our Call
Isaiah 6:8

Chapter 2: Finding Our Purpose
Jeremiah 29:11

Chapter 3: Leadership as Sacred Trust
1 Peter 4:10

Chapter 4: Meetings as Sacred Space
Matthew 18:20

REATREAT 2: STRENGTHENING THE CALL
Ephesians 4:4-6

Chapter 5: Sustaining Leadership
Exodus 17:12

Chapter 6: Governance as Covenant
Nehemiah 9:38

Chapter 7: Making Sense of the Numbers
Luke 16:10

Chapter 8: Faithful Stewardship of Church Resources
2 Corinthians 9:7

ANNIVERSARY REATREAT: SUSTAINING THE VISION
Habakkuk 2:2

Chapter 9: Transparency, Accountability, and Trust
1 Thessalonians 5:21

Chapter 10: Mentoring New Leaders
2 Timothy 2:1–2

Chapter 11: Courage, Compassion, and Commitment
Isaiah 41:10

Chapter 12: A Benediction of Boldness
Joshua 1:9

Leadership Rooted in Discernment

Leadership in church governance is sacred work—rooted not in control, but in listening for God's call. *Serving the Call: Forming Faithful Leaders for Sacred Responsibility* is a practical and Spirit-centered training manual for new governance body members. Designed for 10–17 hours of flexible retreats, Zoom-ready sessions, or monthly meetings, it offers:

- A retreat-based model to build spiritual and practical governance skills
- Tools for unifying mission, finances, and leadership with God's purpose
- Reflection prompts and exercises for communal discernment
- Guidance for trust-building, stewardship, and mentoring future leaders

With warmth, clarity, and real-world wisdom, this manual equips boards to lead with integrity and faith, surpassing standard training in accessibility and mission focus. Accessible to UCC, PC(USA), Disciples, Methodist, and other mainline churches, it's a proven system—join thousands of churches transforming governance.

"This manual transformed our board's approach, blending spiritual depth with practical steps to make governance a true ministry."
— Sarah Thompson, Board Chair, Grace Community Church

Keith Clark-Hoyos is a coach, consultant, and spiritual leader who helps churches align structure and Spirit. With decades of experience in judicatory leadership and nonprofit consulting, he founded Church Training Center to empower faithful governance.

Learn more or join our community at www.ChurchTrainingCenter.com

www.ingramcontent.com/pod-product-compliance
Lightning Source LLC
Chambersburg PA
CBHW080455170426
43196CB00016B/2816